EXAMPLES OF THE INTEGRATION OF TECHNOLOGY IN THE CLASSROOM

ROBERT J. KEALEY, ED.D., EDITOR

DEPARTMENT OF ELEMENTARY SCHOOLS
NATIONAL CATHOLIC EDUCATIONAL ASSOCIATION

ISBN # 1-55833-272-3

CONTENTS

PREFACE

Four years have passed since the NCEA Department of Elementary Schools published *Point to the Future: A Principal's Technology Planning Guide*. In the preface to this book we wrote, "No revolution in education has the power to change American schools so quickly and dramatically as the technological revolution." This four-year period has certainly proven this point.

Point to the Future provided a process for the faculty and staff to integrate technology into the curriculum. Again in that preface we made mention that no two schools are the same. One plan will not fit all situations. Nevertheless schools do find it helpful to have examples of how other schools have integrated technology into the curriculum.

Examples of the Integration of Technology into the Curriculum provides case studies of what some schools have accomplished. NCEA is not saying that these are the best examples. It is merely saying, here's how a few schools developed their plan of technology integration. The title of this book, *Examples of the Integration of Technology into the Curriculum*, reflects this approach. With each selection, readers will notice the variety of approaches because of the differences among schools.

One aspect of these different approaches, however, is common to them all. Teachers need training in how to integrate technology into the curriculum. The principals who wrote these articles took responsibility for this training. Their programs were successful because time and funds were devoted to the training of teachers in this new way of helping students to learn.

The selections in this book were written by some of the participants of the 2000 principals' academy and assistant principals' academy. We are grateful to them for their willingness to share their stories with the entire membership of NCEA.

The NCEA Department of Elementary Schools expresses its gratitude to Janice Kraus, editorial assistant for the department, for her work on the manuscript and to Beatrice Ruiz of the NCEA Computer Graphics Department for designing the cover and laying out the book.

The NCEA Department of Elementary Schools presents this book to the membership with the hope that many school faculties will read it carefully and evaluate their technology integration in light of these examples. It cautions faculties not to think that they can adopt what is stated here but that they can adapt the information to their own situations. Technology does have the power to change the learning situation dramatically and it is our hope that this will result in more effective instruction and deeper learning.

Janet P. Murray, M.A.
President

Robert J. Kealey, Ed.D.
Executive Director

Department of Elementary Schools
National Catholic Educational Association
Feast of St. John Chrysostom, 2001

A PLAN FOR THE INTEGRATION OF TECHNOLOGY

TERESA ANTHONY, M. A., PRINCIPAL
OUR LADY OF MT. CARMEL SCHOOL
REDWOOD CITY, CALIFORNIA

The degree to which a school can successfully integrate computer technology into the curriculum, is dependent on how confident and comfortable teachers feel using computers and other types of technology. Faculty members first need to see how they have been successful in using technology in the classroom. As defined by Webster, technology is an applied science, a technical method of achieving a practical purpose. Teachers across the county have for years been very successful at using technology in their classrooms, but I am not sure they realized that this is what they were doing each time they used an overhead, film or slide projector, TV, VCR, listening center, or video camera. The challenge for administrators is, therefore, to bring this same comfort level of use to the ever-changing technology available today.

The task of administrators is to place a priority on expanding the integration of technology into the curriculum. This needs to be a systematic planned strategy, where faculty members are met "where they are," and then moved to the next level.

TECHNOLOGY PLAN

Schools must have a vision, a plan, and a strategy for why, how, and when technology will be used in the subject areas. The roles teachers will assume will need to be considered as increased integration opportunities. Technology is expensive, but seeking creative financing, taking advantage of grants, partnering with businesses, interfacing with parents in the computer industry, and having sheer determination, will make things happen.

PROFESSIONAL DEVELOPMENT

Paramount to the success of new technologies being used in the classroom, opportunities and funds must be made available to support the school's vision and expectations. With limited resources, I have experimented with many ways to train personnel in the least painful way possible. I have done the following to assist personnel:

- Sent teachers to workshops during the school day,(I found a sub or subbed myself to replace the teacher);
- Brought experts in the field on campus for after-school workshops;
- Allowed teachers to visit other schools during school time;
- Applied for grants;
- Examined the in-service opportunities provided by the county office of education and sent teachers to these programs which are usually very inexpensive;
- Gave time during the school day for teachers to meet with our technology coordinator to discuss problems or strategies on integration;
- Allowed teachers to take school computers home during vacations;
- Purchased a laptop for teachers' use at home or in the classroom.

We need to remember three key points when providing professional development opportunities for faculty:

- Teachers excite teachers;
- Equipment must work;
- Presenters, who are too technical or who don't recognize the level of competency of a faculty, will only frustrate hesitant learners.

TECHNOLOGY GOALS

At the start of the school year, each faculty member must have at least one technology goal. For some, this will be continued professional growth and, for others, it will be using technology to support project-based learning.

Each year, with fair warning, I let faculty and staff know my school-wide technology expectations. These goals have included bringing in a grading program, requiring that written communication going home to all students be word processed, and learning how to use the school's internal e-mail system. As the school's vision of technology grows and expands, so must the administrator's expectation of personnel.

DIOCESAN COMPETENCIES IN TECHNOLOGY

The Catholic schools office in the diocese states that computer enhancement of learning can no longer be ignored. This creates the sense that computer technology is a priority in the diocese and that we must all become computer competent to be effective educators of tomorrow's children.

Teachers are given support from the school's technology coordinator. This person will work with individuals struggling to meet diocesan competencies. Through non-threatening guidance and positive affirmations, all teachers have met yearly competencies.

LESSON PLANS

Checking lesson plans regularly has given me an opportunity to see how the faculty uses technology. During the first year I followed a particular strategy, some points of which are noted:

- The use of any technology in the classroom needs to be highlighted in the lesson plan book. This could be VCR, TV, overhead, listening center, camera, or computers. I monitored the way technology was being used, the type of technology, and the subjects to which it was applied. In conversations with my technology coordinator, we looked for ways to transfer some of this technology to computers. We then began to develop strategies to move a teacher from one type of technology to another, i.e., from displays on the overhead to displays on the large computer monitor.

The second year had a more advanced focus.
- Teachers had to highlight in their lessons plans their use of Internet, classroom computers, lab computers, library computers, scanners, digital cameras, etc.

COMPUTER LAB STRATEGIES

I believe a lab is still essential today because students need to master skills to use the technology available. I don't think there are enough classroom teachers who are yet able to integrate curriculum objectives and computer skills in a classroom with limited computers. Students need practice and understanding of computer skills and computer capabilities, prior to successful, sustained integration. Unless a classroom teacher has a computer for each child or for every two children, it is doubtful that mastery will occur. But once students master basic computer skills, they have a valuable resource to support their learning in the subject areas.

Therefore, classroom teachers should be doing some degree of the following:

- Assisting the technology coordinator to teach computer skills;

- Teaching computer skills themselves;
- Working with the technology coordinators to develop ways in which technology can support the project, activity or presentation expected.

A strategy needs to be developed for the use of the lab in order to see results. After four years of professional development opportunities, technology goals, computers in the classroom, and support from the technology coordinator, the primary-grade teachers are ready and responsible for their students' mastery of grade-level outcomes in computer technology. The middle and junior-high teachers will work on developing projects that are supported by technology. Through projects that are curriculum-driven, developed by the teachers, and supported by the technology coordinator, students will show mastery of grade-level outcomes. Students will still need to be taught the capabilities of the technology, how to use the Internet more efficiently, how to integrate media and how to use technology for the presentation of material learned. They will also be expected to continue to improve their keyboarding skills.

Project-based learning occurs when students, either in a lab setting or a classroom environment, are working on a project. Teachers understand this expectation and see this as a bridge to more integration. When half the class goes to the lab, it is no longer a time for the classroom teacher to work on an unrelated subject.

ROLE OF THE TECHNOLOGY COORDINATOR

To move from the realm of computers being a subject taught by a specialist, to using technology to support the curriculum, the coordinator must:

- Be responsible for overseeing the teacher's involvement in developing grade-level outcomes. Teachers also need to realize that the coordinator is not solely responsible.
- Be present to support and assist teachers. He or she must keep the equipment working and have time built into the schedule to meet with teachers on a regular basis. This must become a cooperative effort. Teachers must be aware of, and experience this support on a consistent basis.
- Ideally, technology coordinators need to be responsible only for technology and the maintenance of equipment.
- Coordinate the acquisition of software.

ADMINISTRATIVE SUPPORT

Computer technology competency for the staff must be a priority. I encourage and expect my staff to continue their professional growth in technology. Thus I am always looking for opportunities for the teachers to attend workshops given by other classroom teachers who have practical, tried methods of successful integration of technology. Teachers motivate teachers. I am supporting the diocesan office and other principals in my areas as they create opportunities to observe teachers integrating technology effectively.

SOFTWARE DEVELOPMENT

Teachers need to be involved in the acquisition of software. A software program that is bought either because it goes along with a textbook series, or is well-advertised, runs the risk of sitting permanently on a shelf. Therefore, teachers

- Need to be given catalogs to review software selections, so that they can order it on a preview basis. My technology coordinator oversees this process, and alerts teachers, by putting software ideas into their mailboxes.
- Are encouraged to attend workshops that review software.
- Are expected to work with previewed software to determine if it is something they may profitably use with their students before it is purchased.
- Consider software that will support the curriculum, that will provide drill and practice, which will facilitate book reports and provide enrichment activities.
- Review software for presentation at all grade levels and purchase after consultation with the technology coordinator and faculty.

CLASSROOM COMPUTERS

At present, we have between one and eight computers in each classroom. They are used in a number of ways:

- Every teacher has one computer connected to the server for internal administrative needs;
- Teachers who are using computers for lesson integration are given a minimum of three machines, printers and scanners;
- Classrooms for fourth-grade and higher level students have the most computers since it is expected that these students will be producing reports and projects and using the Internet for research purposes;
- Teachers who have mastered the use of computers in their classroom are given more machines.

Students in grades four through eight are allowed to use computers in other classrooms. They move quietly into another room to complete the task and save the work to the server. Since all computers are connected to the server, students can now access their work anywhere on campus. This, of course, allows students and teachers flexibility.

As my expectations for technology integration are increasing for classroom teachers, I am now developing a systematic approach to computer allocation in the classrooms. It will no longer be the teacher's choice. Let me summarize my major points:

- For integration of technology to be successful, teachers must be supported by the administration;
- Administrators must make technology integration a priority;
- Strategies need to be put in place so that teachers will be comfortable with technology;
- Every school site must pace its integration to the skills of the classroom teachers, the equipment available, and the expertise of the technology coordinator.

Administrators must never lose sight of the fact that technology supports the curriculum, and that our goal as educators is to improve and enhance student learning. With this basic concept and principle in mind, whatever you do to facilitate this goal will be effective.

INTEGRATING TECHNOLOGY IN THE CLASSROOM

CHARLOTTE BENNETT, PH.D., PRINCIPAL
ST. JOHN SCHOOL
NEWBURGH, INDIANA

O ur technology plan for the school was put into place several years ago, after an assessment was made of the existing equipment. The teaching staff assessed the plan and made suggestions for the technology they wanted and the technology that they thought they needed to make their teaching more effective.

In 1987 we began with one TV and VCR on a cart, three Apple Computers and three overhead projectors. The first thing teachers wanted to have in their classrooms were TV sets and overhead projectors. We made an announcement in the parish bulletin that we were in need of TV sets for the classrooms. On Monday morning, a call came from one of the local hospitals that they would be happy to deliver TV sets for each of the classrooms. The hospital was replacing the big TV sets with bedside sets. Within the next month, after getting the sets, one of our student's parents installed and pulled cable wire to each classroom. Each classroom has the capability of tuning into an all-school video presentation, viewing a separate video or using the closed circuit TV system. Thanks to the contributions of parents and parishioners, all classrooms also have individual VCR's available for use.

The computer lab became a reality when the state made refurbished IBM clone computers available to all schools at a very reduced cost. Our lab was set up to teach keyboarding skills at all levels and to provide practice time for the students, software was also purchased to complement classroom instruction for each grade. This past year, through a special matching grant made available to our parents who work at IBM, we were able to set up a new computer lab that consisted of IBM Pentium II Computers (Windows 98) and IBM laser printers. We also networked the lab so students could send print jobs to one of the various printers. The old computers that were in the lab were placed in the classrooms and the lab was networked with a central file server. Work is now being done to finish wiring the classrooms to the lab and media center.

The services of the library, the central focus of the media center, have been computerized and students check out books using a bar code reader. Computers and printers are also available in the library/media center for research and print jobs.

An IBM scanner and digital camera have been set up for multi-media use in the computer lab. Teachers had requested the capability to take pictures in class or on field trips. These were to be included with written work in stories or in classroom newsletters. Thus the central focus of the multi-media area is to produce and improve student writing activities. The HyperStudio Program is also available in the computer lab to assist in producing projects that students have created in the classrooms.

Our focus on integration of technology in the classroom has always been based on teachers' needs and desires to enrich their instructional techniques. The science teachers were the first to ask for a laser disk reader to accompany their science teaching. The use of this disk reader gave students an overall introduction to the topics being studied and provided an opportunity to look up information and view it on the TV screen.

In several classrooms, the computer has been used as an overhead demonstration for the entire class, using a PC viewer over-head projection device. The students then followed up the demonstration with their own work. An example of this was the dissection of a frog, which was first demonstrated on computer, and then actually dissected. Several other teachers have used this equipment to do Power Point demonstrations for full-class presentations.

Many new interactive materials, in various subject areas, are only available on CD-ROM, which will require upgrades on our existing classroom computers. Most available CD's include interactive materials for the students to use for activities or games with the information that was presented in class. The teacher resource materials and test banks are also on CD-ROM. Our goals for this school year are to upgrade at least one of the 486 computers in each classroom to CD-ROM capability and to add a printer for classroom use.

Our reading test results indicated that comprehension scores were not as high as expected and that our students needed to improve in this area. A search of available leveled reading materials was made to see what programs we could use to increase reading comprehension proficiency.

The Accelerated Reading Program was selected and loaded on all computers from the lab to the classrooms. After each books they read, students have daily access to this program to check their comprehension. This was our first year to use this program; hence, we will measure the effects of the program by using the end-of-the-year reading scores to track growth in comprehension. An online version of this program (Book Adventure at http://www.bookadventure.org) is now available for home and school use and we use this to encourage children to check their comprehension during the evening hours. These two computer programs, Accelerated Reading Program and Book Adventures, are two of the many approaches teachers use to help the students to increase their comprehension skills.

At St. John School we view technology as another teaching tool. Whether it is a camera, TV, computer, or an overhead projection device, our focus is on teaching the subject and not on the technology used. Our curriculum and need drive our technology program.

FROM COMMODORE 64 TO THE MILLENNIUM TECHNOLOGY

ANN HEIDKAMP, M.A., ASSISTANT PRINCIPAL
ST. JULIANA SCHOOL
CHICAGO, ILLINOIS

T he technology being used in education includes computers and other devices as tools in the teaching/learning process. These tools reflect the ways in which technology is used in the workplace and home. A variety of curricular activities use the following tools: word processing programs for writing and revising assignments, graphing programs for mathematics and science instruction, desktop publishing for producing classroom newspapers and school newspapers, and multimedia systems that encourage students to become active learners in their own education.

We at St. Juliana School realize that effective use of these tools is dependent on the perspective, skills and practices of the classroom teacher. Using technology at our school is a process that has evolved since the day we received our first computers. For teachers, computer class was never a free period; they simply participated in the activities and skills that were being taught to the students. Initially, progress was slow, since a limited number of computers were available and classroom teachers were not involved in projects that linked computer technology with their curriculum.

A grant that gave the teachers the opportunity to learn basic and advanced computer skills was the impetus to improving our teacher education program. We knew that unless the teachers developed a more comfortable control of the computer their involvement in integrating technology in the curriculum was limited.

We began an ongoing teacher education program three years ago. In the last two years, we have set up a definite course of study for the teachers (see Appendices A, B, and C). Examples of word processing and use of database and spreadsheets that show the ability to use these programs are now included in their portfolios. Within the first year, 90% of the staff had completed their assignments. Last year we saw a greater involvement of all grades in using technology as one of the tools of learning. HyperStudio was introduced to illustrate how students can become active and engaged learners. We are still working to have our teachers take over the computer instruction so that they control the instructional strategy of providing students with aids for studying particular content or practicing a particular skill, that is, facilitating educational and work-related tasks.

Having computers in every classroom connected to the Internet is another goal. Our six library computers are connected to Internet and last year the students did some research using this tool. This year, twenty-eight of our computers in the lab will be online and we hope to get our student body more involved in research projects. One of our teachers developed her own web page and used it to assist students in her middle-school mathematics class. We also have a school Web page developed by one of our parents. Teachers can use this page to disseminate information to his/her students. Another goal is to have each teacher create a Web page to assist students in their learning.

APPENDIX A: ADDITIONAL TEACHING AGREEMENT

In order to facilitate technology-engaged learning throughout our curriculum at St. Juliana School, you as a faculty member will be asked to commit yourself to a systemic learning program. By the year 2001, you need to be adequately trained in computer literacy so that technology is used as an essential tool in your students' learning. In order to meet this goal, you will be required to embark on a personal training program that integrates your computer skills with the curriculum.

You will be asked to commit yourself to two (2) proficiencies per year. Listed below are the expected skill outcomes. Review them as an individual or with those colleagues with whom you choose to learn. Learning is eclectic and often takes place when the learners are in a comfortable environment. You might want to achieve your goals with a team of teachers. As long as you are able to perform all of the expectations, you will be fulfilling the requirements.

Technology-Engaged Learning Skills Expectations

1. Demonstrate your familiarity and use of a word processing program by composing your teaching goals and teacher portfolio using this tool.

2. Demonstrate your familiarity and use of a spreadsheet document by submitting your class schedule.

3. Demonstrate your familiarity and use with a data base document by submitting a copy of your class list that includes name, address, phone and date of birth.

4. Create a word processing document that includes graphics such as a parent newsletter, classroom news, et.

5. Integrate software into your curriculum. For example:
   Trudy's Time and Place (social studies and math, grades K-3)
   Kids Pix (social studies, reading, language arts for grades k-8)
   ClarisWorks (Grades 1-8)

6. Assisted by the technologist, integrate technology into your curriculum by assigning a word processing, data base, or spreadsheet project to your students.

APPENDIX B:
ST. JULIANA TEACHER'S TECHNOLOGY AND
TEACHING AGREEMENT

Please complete your technology agreement by filling in your anticipated completion dates into column two.

Technology-Engaged Learning Skills	Anticipated Year of Completion	Principal's Signature upon Completion
Work Processing Document: Teacher Goals and Teacher Portfolio		
Spreadsheet Document: Class Schedule		
Database Document: Class List (name, address, phone and date of birth)		
Word Processing Document: Includes Graphics (parent letter, class newsletter, etc.)		
Integrate Software into Curriculum: Choices on previous page. Specify which:		
Assisted by the Technologist: present a lesson/unit incorporating work processing, database or spreadsheet		

Include your signature below as an indication that you have read this agreement.

Teacher Signature: _____

Date: _____

APPENDIX C:
ST. JULIANA TEACHERS' TECHNOLOGY AND TEACHING AGREEMENT FOR
(A)DVANCED (P)LACEMENT (E)NDEAVORS

Please complete your technology agreement by filling in your anticipated completion dates into column two.

Technology-Engaged Learning Skills	Anticipated Year of Completion	Principal's Signature upon Completion
Use and demonstrate inspiration software		
Learn and use Easy Grade Pro to generate progress reports		
Learn and use Easy Grade Pro to generate report card grades		
Learn and demonstrate a slide show presentation		
Integrate technology into curriculum and demonstrate to technology coordinator		
Choose a second project to integrate technology and demonstrate to technology coordinator		

Teacher Signature: _____

Date: _____

A TECHNOLOGY PROJECT FOR EIGHTH GRADERS

ANNA ADAM, M.A.
ASSISTANT PRINCIPAL
ST. JOSEPH SCHOOL
PALM BAY, FLORIDA

Our eighth-grade students needed a project to motivate them during their last term of the school year. Our teaching team discussed what would be an interesting project for students to undertake that would be captivating and educationally beneficial.

Most people are familiar with the science books about Miss Frazzle. In the book the science teacher takes the children on journeys anywhere that they need to go to understand the concept that is being taught. On that same wavelength, we decided to use this idea in the social studies curriculum. Since American history is the topic for the eighth grade curriculum and it covers over one hundred years, we divided the years into decades of time. The social studies teacher, English teacher, technology coordinator and librarian all collaborated to make this project happen.

The students were paired and their first responsibility was to read *Miss Frazzle's Adventures*. Then they chose a time period, any ten-year period from 1840 to 1979. The students were given three periods a week to work on the project. They were told which three periods a week they would work on the project. The following requirements were presented:

- A Power Point presentation of between 15 and 20 slides had to be developed on the decade;
- Five resources were to be used in gathering information for the presentation;
- A bibliography was to be submitted midway through the project.

Each slide needed to be sketched out and have a story line. The first slide would be the title page, and the last slide would be a summary of the trip. There needed to be two slides for each of the following categories: people and events, arts and entertainment, sports, science and technology, and life style. The remaining slides would support the story line.

For their story line, the students were told to think about the characters and their personalities, introduce the characters and name them. The students had to tell how they were to arrive at their destination and explain what they would see, do and possibly hear on their journey. They had to tell a story.

All facts and vocabulary words needed to be written out separately. Each page had to have the vocabulary words woven into the story as well as the chosen facts. On the sketch pages the facts and words had to be highlighted. These pages needed to be numbered. When a vocabulary word was used or a fact presented, the page on which it was found needed to be noted for the teacher. The following example illustrated the point: "A polio vaccine was invented in 1955" (page 5). This indicated to the teacher that this fact would be found on page 5.

After the first session, the two partners submitted their responsibilities. The students might write, "The first student will research people and events, and the partner will research science and technology and life style. Both will research sports and work on the story line." When the students were in the lab or in the library, both were required to hand in what was accomplished during that period, e.g., CD's viewed, sites on the Internet visited. As information was gathered, the weaving of the story line began to emerge.

Power Point has many interesting features that allow the students to be very creative with their illustrations. Many of the students showed just how creative they were by downloading the backgrounds for their slides from the Internet. If students were investigating the inventor of the polio vaccine, for example, the person's face was used on the slide. Or, if someone was explaining who Dr. Martin Luther King, Jr. was, part of one of his speeches might appear on the slide to make it more meaningful. The music teacher provided valuable assistance to the students. As they traveled through time, the students showed whatever vehicle they used and could actually have it zoom across the slide. To do this, the students needed to be fairly proficient in Power Point.

I found the students learned much about their own time period, as well as other time periods because they constantly were on the look out for different things to help each other as they researched. The more specific the teacher was about the information required, the easier it was for the students to begin their research. They really needed to have a handle on Miss Frazzle to understand what was being asked of them.

WE CAN'T SEE THE VISION IF OUR EYES ARE CLOSED

DEBORAH A. SCHWOPE, ASSISTANT PRINCIPAL
RESURRECTION CATHOLIC SCHOOL
LAKELAND, FLORIDA

"Should computer technology be in the classroom?" is about as sensible as questioning the wisdom of Gutenberg's invention (Dusick, 1998). The appropriate question seems to be, "Now that it is there, how do we integrate the use of technology in the classroom?"

Whenever I think of how technology has been introduced and implemented in schools, I am reminded of the movie, "Mr. Mom". In the movie, Michael Keaton's character hops right into the household duties without any preliminary instructions. When he takes his children to school, he enters the drop-off line going in the wrong direction and the crossing guard shouts at him, "You're doing it wrong."

School systems initially began by "doing it wrong," too. I had the privilege of teaching when the Apple Computer was introduced into the classroom in 1985. It was set on the desk (plunk), turned on (click). Throughout the country, the resounding plunk and click was heard, but no training was offered. Little thought was given as to how to use the computer or how it could be integrated into the curriculum. In the hustle and bustle of buying, no planning took place as to how to use the new tool effectively.

Millions of dollars have been spent on hardware, software, and networking, but not as much money or thought has been given to train faculties in the use and integration of computer technologies in the schools. Take, for example, Middle Tennessee State University which spent $50,000 for a digital media center, $100,000 for the three new master classrooms, $35,000/year for a support specialist, and $2.5 million for a campus-wide network (Brace and Roberts, 1997). Out of the $2,685,000 spent, only $35,000 was spent for a support specialist and nothing was spent on staff/faculty training. This is not an isolated incident. School systems across the country have been purchasing equipment without first planning how best to utilize these expenditures. The question is not how computers could improve learning, but how fast could teachers jump on the band-wagon. The "best of the best" of technology has been installed in many schools, but the actual usage has been limping along due to poor planning and faculty training. Faculty training is a pivotal issue in the integration of technology in the classroom. It is not surprising that the success or failure of technology is linked at such a grass roots level, since the teacher becomes the master of his/her environ-ment once the classroom door is closed. Perhaps school systems still don't understand that in order for technology to be used effectively, teachers must become motivated to understand and use it.

What can be done to maximize the possibility that faculties become able to be successful at integrating technology in the class-room? Meckenburger (1989) suggested that administrators play an essential role in the effective use of technology. Lee and Johnson (1998) reported that administrators set the tone for technology inte-gration, articulating a vision and supporting integration. Hoffman (as cited in Lee & Johnson, 1998, p. 16) stated that successful staff development could take as long as three to five years. School systems that made the initial investment in the hardware must now empha-size the training of the faculty. Pryor and Bitter (1995-96) cited a nationwide study of K-12 teachers and found that 59% of respon-dents believed that most teachers were inadequately trained in com-puter usage.

Leggett and Persichitte (as cited in Schrum, 1995) identified four barriers to increased telecommunications usage: time, access, resources, and expertise. The authors added a fifth component, support, to the barriers. Assuming that school systems are providing the access and resources, it is left to the individual school and teachers to find the time, invest in qualified expertise, and provide support in both the administrative and technical aspects of techno-logical integration.

In my opinion, a three-tiered system is needed in order for the integration of technology to be successful. The following outline illustrates what I see as the responsibilities of each tier.

Tier I – Arch/Diocesan School Office
- Sets standards for administrators and teachers in technol-ogy.
- Provides/updates appropriate infrastructure.
- Develops a strategic plan for technology.
- Provides ongoing teacher education.

Tier II – School Administration
- Conducts a needs' assessment.

- Develops realistic faculty expectations.
- Sets the tone for technology integration.
- Provides ongoing and extensive guidance and support.
- Articulates a technology vision.
- Provides teacher inservice throughout the year.
- Sets an example by using technology.

Tier III – School Faculty
- Takes time to become familiar with technology.
- Participates in on-site instruction.
- Attends in-service training.
- Takes college courses.
- Accepts coaching from "techies".
- Attends conferences.
- Pursues advanced courses.
- Integrates technology into teaching style.
- Develops an understanding of personal teaching style.
- Adapts to change.

When there is a breakdown in one of the tiers, success will be difficult, if not impossible, to achieve. The school diocesan office, school administration and school faculty must work as a cohesive team in order to achieve results.

Eastwood, Harmony, and Chamberlain (1998) discussed a New York school district whose original method of technology was the plunk and clink method where computers were dumped into the classrooms. The school district had failed to consider that teachers needed guidance and direction with technology integration. For years the schools failed to create resource-rich classrooms even though the technology existed right in the classroom itself. Then, in 1994-95, they began a process to implement a strategic plan to improve the usage of computer technology and educate faculty. With this newfound vision, they were able to chart a course for success. Instrumental in the success of the program was providing staff development and attending to the unique needs of the faculty. Benchmarks for teachers were established and wide arrays of enrichment courses were offered.

Universities and colleges, too, must take responsibility for preparing prospective teachers to use technology as an integral part of their instruction. Zachariades, Jenson and Thompson (1997) cite a national survey that shows more than 50% of teachers who graduated within the last two years were not prepared or were poorly prepared to use technology in their instruction. Schools of higher learning must take the initiative to provide education that includes technology application for aspiring teachers. Falling down on this issue puts school systems continuously "behind the eight ball" by having constantly to teach basic concepts to beginning teachers.

In summary, the success of technology integration depends on each level of the school system including schools of higher learning. By developing a strategic plan, diocesan school offices illumine the vision for the school administrators. They, in turn, set the tone of integration for their particular school by articulating and providing a reliable learning environment for their faculty. The school faculty must take the time to develop an understanding of technology and how to integrate it into the curriculum. In the end, the students of the future are the winners. These children do not know what the world was like before computer technology. In many aspects of their world, technology is king. School systems and teachers must develop the vision to supply the tools for the students to succeed.

BIBLIOGRAPHY

Brace, S.J. & Roberts, G. (1997). When Payup Becomes Payback: A University's Return on Instructional Technology Investment. *Syllabus*, 11 (1), 30-37.

Brandt, P. W. and Bitter, G. G. (1995-96). Lessons Learned for Integrating Technology into Teacher Education. *Journal of Computing in Teacher Education*. 12(2), 16-18.

Dusick, D. M. (1998). The Effectiveness of Education Technology: What Does That Really Mean? *Educational Technology Review*, 10, 10-12.

Eastwood, K. W., Harmony, D., & Chamberlain, C. (1998). Opening the Electronic Doorway into Classrooms: How One School District Joined the Technology Revolution. *Learning and Leading with Technology*, 16, (1) 48-52.

Lee, J. R. & Johnson, C. (1998). Helping Higher Education Faculty Clear Instructional Technology Hurdles. *Educational Technology Review*, 10, 10-12.

Leggett, W. P., & Persichitte, K. A. (1998). Blood, Sweat and TEARS: 50 Years of Technology Implementation Obstacles. *Techtrends*, 43(3), 33-36.

Mecklenburger, J. (1989). Technology in the 1990's: Ten Secrets for Success. *Principal*, 69(2) 6-8. Two Miles Down a Ten Mile Road. Counsel for School Performance (April 5, 1999). *http://cspweb.gsu.edu/csp/csp_instrtech.htm*

Zachariades, E. H., Jenson, S.I., & Thompson, A. (1998). One-on-One Collaboration with a Teacher Educator: An Approach to Teacher Education. *Journal of Computing in Teacher Education*, 12(1), 11-14.

THE IMPORTANCE OF STAFF DEVELOPMENT IN TECHNOLOGY

SISTER M. EILEEN BARROW, OP, PRINCIPAL
SCHOOL OF ST. ELIZABETH
NEW YORK, NEW YORK

MISSION STATEMENT

Educating the whole child for full life is the philosophy of St. Elizabeth School. We believe that the quality of education our students receive is critical in preparing them for the challenges awaiting them, and we must anticipate their future needs when designing our curriculum. One such need is technology, which has become an integral part of our society during the past decade. One's ability to use computers will become increasingly important and essential for success in the future workplace.

St. Elizabeth School has long believed that computer literacy is a necessary fundamental skill for our students. We know that technology can be a powerful tool for enhancing the educational curriculum. Our vision for technology includes building a learning environment where technology is integrated into every subject area in every classroom and all students have equitable access to computers. Such an infusion of technology, together with ongoing staff training, will better prepare our students for the Information Age. Since 1995, we have invested much time researching and carefully formulating a comprehensive long-term plan to implement our technology goals. This plan includes the technology goals submitted to the Middle States Association of Colleges and Schools as part of St. Elizabeth School's Sixth Year Periodic Review.

STAFF DEVELOPMENT

We believe that the single most important element in the school's Technology Plan is the training of teachers in the use of technology. Teachers are the most important component in the educational environment, and their comfort level with technology is crucial in the integration of technology into the curriculum. Therefore, we are committed to providing administrators, faculty and staff with the opportunity for ongoing technology training.

As a joint recipient of the 1997, 1998 and 1999 New York State Learning Technology Grants, in collaboration with New York City Public School 128, St. Elizabeth School receives twelve days of on-site professional development each year. All teachers participated in the training that included workshops and one-on-one sessions with a professional developer. All sessions were custom designed according to the skill levels of the participants. The professional developer also worked on-site in the classrooms with the teachers of Kindergarten and Grades five through eight in 1998–1999. This opportunity will be extended to the teachers of Grades one through four in 1999-2000. In addition, through a grant from the Patrons Program of the Archdiocese of New York, twenty additional days of on-site training are provided by Teaching Matters, Inc., 475 Riverside Drive, N.Y. Moreover, all teachers attend weekly computer lab sessions with their students. Computer classes were also available after school for both teachers and students.

FUNDING SOURCES

In addition to the revenue received from the NYS Technology Grants (1997-1999), the following sources provide the financial support necessary to implement and maintain the program:

- St. Elizabeth School Advisory Board
- Grants
- Annual Appeal
- Technology Fee ($50 per student)

CURRENT INVENTORY

The first steps toward building a new Technology Center were taken in 1995. Advice was sought from numerous sources to formulate a design that would best meet our needs and construction was begun in July 1996. During 1996-97, a raised modular floor with built-in electrical outlets was installed. This allowed all wiring to be easily hidden and the modular panels rearranged to accommodate various computer configurations. New electrical lines were installed to meet the anticipated demand of the lab; computer tables and chairs, ergonomically designed and height-adjustable, were acquired; and a new air conditioning system was installed.

When the 1997-98 academic year began, St. Elizabeth School had in place a multimedia technology center, equipped with thirty networked Pentium student workstations, four networked printers, including a high-speed LaserJet, a color DeskJet and a teacher's workstation. This workstation is connected to a 32" TV, through a PC-TV adapter, for instruction and presentations and served as the teacher's file server.

Throughout the school, there are eight multimedia Pentium computers, five DeskJet printers, which are distributed in eight classrooms and eight TV/VCR units. Kindergarten through Grade Three classrooms are equipped with one Pentium workstation. There are also three Pentium computers and three Macintosh computers located in the offices for administrative tasks.

All new computers have ClarisWorks 4.0 for Windows 95, which includes word processing, spreadsheet, database, drawing and slide show features. There is a collection of software available for use by teachers, staff and students.

SCHOOL TECHNOLOGY GOALS AND OBJECTIVES

The school's technology goals for 1999-2002 are:

- Equip every classroom with computers. During classroom activities, the students will have the opportunity to apply the skills they have learned in the computer lab and to reinforce these skills independently. Peer teaching will be encouraged by classroom teachers.

- Acquire additional software. In addition to the basic application tool software, subject and task-specific programs are needed to enhance the educational curriculum.

- Establish a Library Multimedia Reference Center complete with CD-ROMs and supervised on-line access to the World Wide Web. The students will gain valuable research skills as well as learn how to access and evaluate information in an age that offers such vast amounts of data.

- Network the school to provide electronic communication throughout the building. With central-server computers, all students and teachers will be able to access their work from anywhere in the building, eliminating the need to transmit work on floppy disks or paper. Memos, notices, and other messages can be sent or posted electronically, improving communication as well as reducing paper usage.

- Enable Internet access from all computers. The teachers will be able to incorporate information available on the World Wide Web into their classroom instruction. The students will be able to communicate with other groups regardless of distance and even observe distant sites using videoconferencing capabilities.

ADDITIONAL EQUIPMENT REQUIRED TO ACHIEVE GOALS

Classroom Computers
- 40 Multimedia Computers
- 20 Printers and peripherals
- Software
- 8 TV-PC Adapters
- Electrical Wiring

School-wide Network
- 1 Network Server Computer
- 24 Hubs
- Network Cables and Wiring
- Network Software
- Network Installation and Maintenance Contract

Additional Software
- Software
- Volume licenses

Library Reference Center
- 5 Multimedia Computers
- Network and Communications Server
- Reference CDs
- Telephone Lines
- Internet Access Accounts
- Printers and peripherals
- Electrical Wiring

School-wide Internet Access
- School-wide Network
- Communications Server
- Telephone Lines
- Internet Access Accounts

EXPECTED RESULTS

Successful implementation of this Technology Plan will create a school where:

- technology is fully integrated into educational curriculum;
- the average student-to-computer ratio is 8:1;
- every student has equitable access to computers and the Internet;
- every student and teacher is comfortable using technology and is computer literate;

- the learning environment is interactive;
- communication is improved between teachers and students, among students, and among the staff;
- the boundless amount of information available on the World Wide Web can be used for education;
- the students are trained to access and evaluate information.

EVALUATION

The implementation and success of this Technology Plan can be evaluated by:

- the number of multimedia computers in the school;
- the number and the volume of new software titles available;
- the number of students and teachers who are proficient in using computers;
- the number of curriculum areas in which classroom computers are integrated;
- the number of programs in which the students and teachers are proficient;
- the number of classrooms with Internet access;
- the number of students who can "navigate" the Internet;
- the increased number of collaborative projects, including student newspapers, yearbook and literary publications.

FOR MORE INFORMATION CONTACT:

Middle States Association of Colleges and Schools at
http//www.ces-msa.org
or
St. Elizabeth School at Hope187@aol.com.

APPENDIX A
TECHNOLOGY PLAN BUDGET

CLASSROOM COMPUTERS
(Purchase Distributed Over 3 Years)

Item Description	Unit Price	Quantity	Year1 Cost	Year2 Cost	Year3 Cost
Multimedia Computer w/ Installation	$1,900	40	$22,800	$24,700	$24,700
Printer and Peripherals	$400	20	$2,400	$2,800	$2,800
Printer Cartridges	$30	90	$600	$900	$1,200
Basic Software	$200	40	$2,400	$2,600	$2,600
Educational Software			$2,000	$5,000	$5,000
TV-PC Adapters	$250	8	$2,000		
Classroom Computer Total Cost			**$32,200**	**$36,000**	**$36,300**

STAFF DEVELOPMENT

Item Description	Unit Price	Quantity	Year1 Cost	Year2 Cost	Year3 Cost
On-Site Professional Development	$520	20	$10,400	$10,400	$10,400
Total Annual Cost (Excluding Network)			**$42,600**	**$46,400**	**$46,700**

SCHOOL WIDE NETWORK/INTERNET ACCESS

Item Description	Unit Price	Quantity	Year1 Cost	Year2 Cost	Year3 Cost
Network Server Computer – Classrooms	$6,000	1	$6,000		
(e.g., Pentium II, 128 MB RAM,					
Backup Tape Drive, Windows NT)					
Communications Server & Software	$2,000	1	$2,000		
Hubs – Classrooms	$150	20	$3,000		
Hubs – Floors	$500	4	$2,000		
Electrical Wiring	$1,000	20	$20,000		
Network Router	$2,000	1	$2,000		
Network Wiring and Installation			$8,000		
Network Software			$2,000		
Network Maintenance (Annual)			$5,000	$5,000	$5,000
Telephone Lines (Annual)	$400	10	$4,000	$4,000	$4,000
Internet Access Accounts (Annual)	$240	10	$2,400	$2,400	$2,400
Total Network/Internet Cost	**$56,400**		**$11,400**	**$11,400**	
Universal Service School Budget Required			*$5,640*	*$1,140*	*$1,140*

LIBRARY REFERENCE CENTER

Item Description	Unit Price	Quantity	Year1 Cost	Year2 Cost	Year3 Cost
Multimedia Computer w/ Installation	$1,900	5	$9,500		
Network Server Computer	$6,000	1	$6,000		
Communications Server	$2,000	1	$2,000		
Hubs – Library	$500	1	$500		
Communications Server & Software	$2,000	1	$2,000		
Reference CDs	$50	10	$500	$500	$500
Printer and Peripherals	$400	5	$400	$800	$800
Telephone Lines (Annual)	$400	5	$2,000	$2,000	$2,000
Internet Access Accounts (Annual)	$240	5	$1,200	$1,200	$1,200
Electrical Wiring	$1,000	1	$1,000		
Library Ref. Center Total Cost			**$25,100**	**$4,500**	**$4,500**
Universal Service School Budget Required			***$11,060***	***$1,620***	***$1,620***

	Year1	Year2	Year3
Total Annual Cost	**$124,100**	**$62,300**	**$62,600**
Total Annual Cost (w/ Universal Service)	**$59,300**	**$49,160**	**$49,460**

BEST PRACTICES IN INTEGRATION OF TECHNOLOGY

SUSAN POETZEL, M.A.T., ASSISTANT PRINCIPAL
ST. GILES SCHOOL
OAK PARK, ILLINOIS

I t was with a sense of shock and great jubilation that Mrs. Constance Schwab, principal, opened the letter from *Today's Catholic Teacher* announcing that St. Giles had been selected for the 1999 Catholic Schools for Tomorrow/Innovations in Technology Award. As St. Giles continues to progress with its technology plan, the technology resource staff and teachers have focused on making technology a visibly integrated component of the curriculum across the grade levels. Technology instruction and integration focuses on basic skills, word-processing, database, spreadsheet, multimedia programs and Internet usage.

St. Giles' campus consists of three classroom buildings, each of which has a technology resource staff and a Power Macintosh lab. In the primary unit, first and second-grade students each have weekly computer/library time ranging from 75–100 minutes. A monthly calendar of curriculum topics is shared with the resource teacher, who plans collaborative and supportive tasks to be done with the computer. For various reports, students research their topics using a CD-ROM encyclopedia and other software, then type and print out their reports. For Christmas, paired students used a drawing program to create an animal or figure for the unit's manger scene display. As a culminating activity, the second-graders produced a ClarisWorks slide show about their trip to the Shedd Aquarium.

In the third and fourth grades similar technology integration is achieved. Students have a weekly 45-minute computer session as well as use of the lab for ongoing curriculum projects. At this level, word processing skills are further developed and students also use multimedia and scanning to create a slide show on the planets. In addition, basic keyboarding is taught and practiced. To facilitate further technology integration, all the labs are equipped with a mobile cart mini-computer lab, consisting of a computer, scanner, printer, presenter, and TV that can be moved into the classroom.

In the Fifth to Eighth-Grade units, the computer lab is equipped with Power Macintosh machines, two scanners, Internet access on one machine (the entire lab will be networked this fall), a Quickcam, and a digital camera. Students have a weekly 45-minute computer session and are scheduled as needed to complete ongoing projects. The lab is available to students before and after school and during lunch. Whenever a computer skill is introduced and practiced, it is integrated with a curriculum project that is planned jointly with the various teachers. Students develop spreadsheet skills by working on a budget, baseball statistical analysis, and a grade book for Seventh and Eighth Grade math classes. A database of artists with student-written vitae was coordinated with the Eighth Grade Master Painting project.

St. Giles has excelled in the use of multimedia and technology skills integrated with the curriculum. Over the past three years, projects have included slide show technology for projects on the Middle Ages, famous religious structures, diseases, space exploration, frog anatomy (after using the program Operation Frog) and endangered animals. In addition, Hyperstudio presentations are used for assessment in producing an autobiography project called "What I Did This Summer—Multimedia Style"(see Appendix A) and in other projects, such as Women in History and America in the Twentieth Century. The presentations are equally helpful when students study the pre-Civil War period and the Vietnam War (see Appendix B).

One outstanding project, for which St. Giles received the Innovations in Technology Award, was the Eighth-Grade study of the Illinois Constitution. This multifaceted, technology-rich project was enhanced by the school's participation in Project Connect, a Technology Challenge Literacy Fund Grant coordinated through Oak Park River Forest High School. As the students were finishing their textbook study of the Constitution, they took a trip to Springfield to visit the state capital and other state historical sites. During the trip, two students were in charge of taking photos with digital camera equipment that would later be used in projects based on this trip. Back in the classroom, students were given their assignments. Each of the two eighth- grade social studies classes became the Illinois General Assembly (the name of the Illinois Legislature). Students served as state senators or representatives and formed committees to research and write bills. These bills were presented to the General Assembly via digital projection of ClarisWorks slide show programs. Other groups of students used digital photos to create a travel guide for each site to be displayed at conferences and to be incorporated into a page for the St. Giles Web site.

The resource staff and teachers have learned some useful

lessons about the preparation, implementation, and assessment of multi-media projects. In order for such a program to be successful:

- Teachers must have stated curriculum and technology objectives for the project;
- Teachers must have a realistic time allotment for project completion;
- Students must have a clear idea of project requirements;
- Stacks, cards, and slides should be researched and planned before the student begins to use the multi-media program;
- For multimedia programs without word processing tasks, students should type text in a word processing program first, allowing for editing help, and then transfer the text into the multimedia program;
- A limit should be placed on the number of scanned images permitted so that students are encouraged to use other graphic/drawing aspects of the multimedia program;
- Rubrics should be encouraged as a useful tool for assessment (see Appendix C for a rubric developed for an eighth-grade social studies project and Appendix D for a more generic HyperStudio rubric).

One area in which St. Giles plans to expand its technology integration is the Internet. In the past, web sites have been bookmarked for various research projects and used in conjunction with other sources. This year, having a networked lab with Internet access will enable more students to use this resource. Two years ago, our Seventh-Grade students designed and constructed our school web site (*www.math.uic.edu/stgiles*). Eighth-Grade students update the site monthly and post the junior high homework assignments for the Homework Hotline daily. Using e-mail to consult experts and collaborate on projects with other schools will be helpful in integrating technology into the curriculum. This year, St. Giles' Fifth Grade will take part in a Technology Literacy Challenge Grant coordinated by the Oak Park Elementary School District. The focus of the grant is to integrate the reading of historical fiction with the social studies curriculum. The grant also allows students to produce various forms of writing based on their studies that will be shared on an electronic database with students from other schools in Oak Park. In addition, the junior high school students will be collaborating to plan and implement a millennium project through e-mail with a school in Oak Park, Michigan.

Technology is an instructional tool, but it also has become an integral and growing part of our students' lives. For that reason, it is important that technology is integrated into the learning environment, not as an add-on, but as part of a seamless system of preparing our students for the information age.

APPENDIX A
WHAT I DID THIS SUMMER—MULTIMEDIA STYLE

"What I did this summer" is a computer project in which you will

- learn how to organize information for a HyperStudio project;
- learn how to create a multimedia HyperStudio stack;
- review how to scan photographs, objects;
- review how to write an informative paragraph;
- review how to make a presentation using the computer.

You will receive a grade on this **project** that will apply to your computer and language arts grades.

You will receive a grade on your **presentation** that will apply to your computer and language arts grades.

Directions:
1. Use the planning sheets to organize your HyperStudio stack. Your stack will have four or five cards.
2. Card one will have title, your name, photos.
3. Card two will contain background information about the trip/event: when, where, who went or participated, how you traveled, weather, etc. (Use one paragraph).
4. Card three/four will list details about the topic. You can use a photo or other scanned item; you may need another card. (Use one paragraph).
5. Card five: Conclusion or brief statement: what you liked or didn't like about your experience; would you try it again/ why? (Use one paragraph)

Be sure to include any words you want to use and note any artwork, photos, or objects in the planning sheet.

When your planning sheet is done AND APPROVED, you can start on your own HyperStudio stack.

Text will be written in ClarisWorks and transferred into your HyperStudio stack.

It is very important that you save your work often.
When you finish your cards, check them over for any mistakes.

Practice your presentation for the class.

APPENDIX B
THE VIETNAM WAR

Steps to the Project:

Research:
1. Your research notes will be collected and graded. You should follow the usual note-taking format. You must use at least two sources.
2. Put title, author, and copyright for each reference.
3. Using left margin line, put main ideas on left side of line, put details on right of the line.
4. To be eligible for an A grade, you must also meaningfully incorporate some ideas from primary sources either in your card script or in your oral script.

Design and Construction of HyperStudio Stack:
You will work during social studies class and use computer time to design and produce your show. The stack must consist of at least six cards.

Card 1: the title and your name.

Cards 2-5: Divide your topic into four meaningful subtopics consisting of a short script and graphic or scanned picture. Use only one scanned picture.

Card 6 or last card: conclusion to your topic. State its importance or significance during the war and/or today.

Quiz on the topic: You must design a 10-question quiz based on your HyperStudio presentation. (No word searches)

Oral presentation of HyperStudio Stack: The completed stack and presentation will be a test grade. Criteria:
1. Organization of slide show
2. Thoroughness of information
3. Creative use of graphics/pictures/drawings
4. Correct grammar and spelling in text
5. Ability to explain the topic and to answer questions by teacher and students

APPENDIX C
HYPERSTUDIO EVALUATION RUBRIC

Name: _____

Topic: _____

Requirements:	Excellent	Good	Adequate	Poor
Meaningful use of Primary Sources needed (to be eligible for "A")	Integrates primary sources within topic analysis	Uses primary sources as an add-on to analysis	Uses primary sources with weak connections to the topic	No primary sources cited
In-class research notes	Organizes notes; Demonstrates research effort; sources identified	Good start on notes but needs more; sources not identified	Few notes for amount of time allotted for research	Notes not turned in
Organization: Title card, 4 subtopic cards, analysis card	All Requirements met	Good title and subtopic cards; weak or missing analysis card	Subtopic cards poorly organized; weak or missing analysis	Not organized according to requirements
Thoroughness of information- text	Text superbly explains topic with research facts, events, and primary sources	Text explains topic well with researched facts and events.	Text moderately explains topic with researched facts and events	Text weakly explains topic with researched facts and events.
Effective use of graphics, drawings, pictures, sounds	Graphics superbly integrate with text and topic	Graphics support well the text and topic	Graphics moderately support text and topic	Graphics weakly support text and topics
Grammar and spelling	Only 1 or 2 mistakes	Only 3-5 mistakes	Only 6-8 mistakes	Many mistakes
Oral Presentation	Without relying on notes, Demonstrated knowledge of the topic	Demonstrated knowledge of topic; relied some on notes	Relied heavily on notes; difficulty explaining aspects of the topic	Demonstrated little knowledge of topic; unable to answer questions

HyperStudio Social Studies/Computer Project Evaluation

Name: _____   Grade: _____

A	B	C	D	F
Excellent class cooperation. Always listens. Always gives best effort.	Good class cooperation. Follows directions. Gives best effort.	Little class cooperation. Does not always listen, follow directions, give best effort.	No class cooperation. Does not listen, follow directions, give best effort.	No class cooperation. Does not listen, follow direction, give best effort.
Excellent completed project with title, introduction, 5 topic cards, and conclusion.	Good completed project with title card, introduction, 5 topic cards and conclusion.	Fair project with title card and at least 6 other cards.	Poor project 3 or less cards completed.	No cards completed.
Title card is excellent. Color, use of graphics, font and music all work together.	Title card is well designed. Color, use of graphics, font and music all work together.	Title card is designed, color, use of graphics, font and music work somewhat together.	Title card is poorly designed. Color, use of graphics, font and music do not work together.	Title card is not designed. Color, use of graphics, font and music do not work together.
Excellent conclusion card that supports the other cards and the topic	Good conclusion card that supports the other cards and the topic	Fair conclusion card that somewhat supports the other cards and the topic.	Poor conclusion card that does not support the other cards and the topic	No conclusion card.
Excellent creative use of graphics that fit with topic of stack	Good creative use of graphics that fit with topic of stack	Fair creative use of graphics that somewhat fit with topic of stack.	Poor creative use of graphics that do not fit with topic of stack	No creative use of graphics
Excellent creative use of sound that fits with topic of stack	Good creative use of sound that fits with topic of stack	Fair creative use of sound that fits with topic of stack	Poor creative use of sound that fits with topic of stack	No creative use of sound
Shows excellent knowledge of HyperStudio	Shows good knowledge of HyperStudio	Shows some knowledge of HyperStudio	Shows little knowledge of HyperStudio	Shows no knowledge of HyperStudio

TECHNOLOGY 2000

**LINDA S. HIXON, M.S., ASSISTANT PRINCIPAL
ST. THOMAS THE APOSTLE SCHOOL
ELKHART, INDIANA**

Technology at St. Thomas has been in the formation stage for years. Finding the funds for this project has been our major stumbling block. Finally in 1998, as a result of performance-based accreditation (PBA), which are standards issued by the state of Indiana, we found something had to be done if we were going to survive. A technology committee was formed and a plan was developed. The committee envisioned the following:

- Administrators, teachers, and students should become proficient in the use of technology with an understanding of the implications of its usage.
- Technology should be used as a vehicle of communication, analysis, and research in the light of values and moral decision-making.
- Students of St. Thomas the Apostle School will have the opportunity to enhance their learning by effective use of technology throughout their educational program.

Goals that were established and put into place are as follows.

PROFESSIONAL DEVELOPMENT

All staff members acknowledge the importance of professional development as a key to successful integration of technology. Among the teachers there is diversity in technology skills and proficiencies. Professional development opportunities for technology, therefore, must address this diversity.

Summer classes have been provided through the diocese for teachers who want to become more computer-literate. These classes can be taken for any additional credits necessary to maintain state licenses. Teachers who are already more computer literate hold after-school classes for those who find the computer a true learning disability.

Computers and software are available to teachers during the summer for those who want to familiarize themselves with the material.

CURRICULUM DEVELOPMENT

- Teachers will incorporate technology into the curriculum and utilize it as a learning tool. They are given brochures and information of upcoming workshops and seminars throughout the year. These workshops are intended to aid the teacher in implementing the use of computers in the curriculum.
- Students at each grade level will have access to a variety of technological equipment in their learning (See attached worksheets).
- Students are given a variety of opportunities to demonstrate proficiency of technological skills.
- Software purchases support continuous integration of technology within the curriculum.
- Teachers will evaluate resource materials provided by textbook publishers in the current year of adoption and select products that will enrich their curriculum.
- Software supports grade-level skills development as found in the Diocesan Technology Plan (See Appendix A).
- Students will go to the computer lab two or three times a week to develop necessary skills.
- Teachers may work with the lab instructor to develop cross-curriculum ideas.
- Teachers will have the ability to access the Internet to incorporate and enrich subject lessons.

HARDWARE

Hardware purchases will support continuous integration of technology within the curriculum. To date, all classrooms have at least one computer and the computer lab has new PC's. The library has three computers and is connected to the Internet. It should be noted that students would have control on use of the Internet. Parents will be made aware of these controls. While not operative at this time, classroom computers are being connected to the central office. When connections are complete, teachers will be able to record absences and submit grades directly to the office.

The students will have access to the classroom computer to work on projects or complete homework assignments. In the past, St. Thomas the Apostle School has not had a systematic approach to technology. Since the drafting of our plan, technology has become a vital part of the curriculum planning and parish budget. In the school year 1999-2000, a technology fee of $50.00 was added. This money will provide new upgrades, software, and hardware. For the current school year, many new advances have come about because of this money.

In addition to computers, other technological advances have been made. We have a digital camera for teacher and student use. Pictures of various events are taken and used in our parent newsletter and parish bulletin. Parishioners are more aware of the activities in the school and can better relate to them. Classrooms have access to TV/VCR's, videotapes and video cameras. These materials are to be checked out through the media specialist, the librarian. There has been discussion of the purchasing of wall TV's for each classroom once we are cable-ready. As media specialist, the librarian is able to update materials in the library such as videos and computer software. Our librarian has found different organizations, government monies, or grants to help improve our program.

Teachers are making use of television programming through CNN, A&E, Discovery Channel, and the History Channel. Publications are received and reviewed for curriculum compatibility. Some channels will send out lesson plans to be used in connection with their programming. Teachers are encouraged to make use of these resources. When the money becomes available, all classrooms will be cable-ready and have access to the Internet.

St. Thomas the Apostle School has not had a systematic approach to technology implementation. We have pieced "bytes and parts" together to get into the age of computers. The plan was a start. It produced a timeline and is working and growing. Our principal is computer literate and innovative. With his background, technology at St. Thomas took off. More has been accomplished in eighteen months than in the last five years. He took the plan from talk to action.

APPENDIX A
MAKING CONNECTIONS – DRAFT 2
DIOCESAN TECHNOLOGY PLAN AND GUIDELINES
PROFILE FOR TECHNOLOGY LITERATE STUDENTS
IN GRADES 6-8

Performance indicators:

All students should have opportunities to demonstrate the following performances.

Prior to completion of grade eight, students will:

1) Apply strategies for identifying and solving routine hardware and software problems that occur during everyday use (1)

2) Demonstrate knowledge of current changes in information technologies and the effect those changes have on workplace and society. (2)

3) Exhibit legal and ethical behaviors when using information and technology, and discuss consequences of misuse (2)

4) Use content-specific tools, software and simulations (e.g., environmental probes, graphing calculations, exploratory environments, Web tools) to support learning and research. (3,5)

5) Apply productivity/multimedia tools and peripherals to support personal productivity, group collaboration, and learning throughout the curriculum. (3,6)

6) Design, develop, publish and present products (e.g., Web pages, video tapes) using technology resources that demonstrate and communicate curriculum concepts to audiences inside and outside the classroom. (4,5, 6)

7) Collaborate with peers, experts, and others using telecommunications and collaborative tools to investigate curriculum-related problems, issues, and information and to develop solutions or products for audiences inside and outside the classroom (4,5)

8) Select and use appropriate tools and technology resources to accompany a variety of tasks and solve problems. (5,6)

9) Demonstrate an understanding of concepts underlying hardware, software, and connectivity, and practical applications to learning and problem solving. (1,6)

10) Research and evaluate the accuracy, relevance, appropriateness, comprehensiveness, and bias of electronic information sources concerning real-world problems. (2,5,6)

Numbers in parenthesis following each performance indicator refer to the standards category to which the performance is linked.

The standard categories are:

1.	Basic operations and concepts
2.	Social, ethical and human issues
3.	Technology productivity tools
4.	Technology communications tools
5.	Technology research tools
6.	Technology problem-solving and decision-making tools

APPENDIX B
CURRICULUM DEVELOPMENT

Topics	Knowledge Compre-hensiion	Application	Analysis	Synthesis	Evaluation
Graphic Activity					
Word Processing Activity					
Date Base Activity					
Spread Sheet Activity					

APPENDIX C
INTEGRATING TECHNOLOGY WITHIN THE CURRICULUM
WHAT DOES IT LOOK LIKE WHEN IT HAPPENS?

Performance Indicator	Class/subject Specify grade level	Sample activity Describe a lesson in which technology is used.	Thinking Skill From Bloom's Taxonomy

TECHNOLOGY CURRICULUM

PATRICIA PREROST, M.S. ED., PRINCIPAL
ST. CATHERINE OF SIENA SCHOOL
LAGUNA BEACH, CALIFORNIA

The following is the technology plan for St. Catherine of Siena School. This plan has been developed over the years and was written as a formal report during the 1998-1999 school year. A committee of faculty members worked on the project. The plan included: school-wide goals for technology use, grade-level objectives, and standards for technology use, as well as technology skill standards, the variety of teaching strategies used, assessment techniques used, grading policies, and the integration of technology in other areas for student learning in addition to the actual classroom.

SCHOOL-WIDE GOALS

To succeed in our information-rich world, students must be able to use technology effectively to access the information available to them. Our students, enabled by an integrated approach to technology and curriculum, should be:
- Informed, responsible, and contributing citizens,
- Creative and effective users of productivity tools,
- Communicators, collaborators, publishers, producers, information seekers, analyzers, and evaluators.

GRADE-LEVEL OBJECTIVES TO IMPLEMENT SCHOOL GOALS

Student standards, skills and outcomes for technology use in Grades K-8 have been adopted from the *Technology Curriculum Guidelines* from the Diocese of Orange and *Tech Works Skills Curriculum* from Teacher Created Materials, Inc.

Standards for Technology use:

1. **Basic operation and concepts:** Students demonstrate a sound understanding of the nature and operation of technology systems; students are proficient in the use of technology.

2. **Social, ethical, and human issues:** Students understand the ethical, cultural, and societal issues related to technology; students practice responsible use of technology systems, information, and software; students develop positive attitudes toward technology uses that support lifelong learning, collaboration, personal pursuits and productivity.

3. **Technology productivity tools:** Students use technology tools to enhance learning, increase productivity, and promote creativity; students use productivity tools to collaborate in constructing other creative works.

4. **Technology communication tools:** Students use telecommunications to collaborate, publish, and interact with peers, experts, and other audiences; students use a variety of media and formats to communicate information and ideas effectively to multiple audiences.

5. **Technology research tools:** Students use technology to locate, evaluate, and collect information from a variety of sources; students use technology tools to process data and report results; students evaluate and select new information resources and technological innovations based on their appropriateness for specific tasks.

6. **Technology problem-solving and decision-making tools:** Students use technology resources for solving problems and making informed decisions; students employ technology in the development of strategies for solving problems in the real world.

Technology Skill Strands:

1. General technology awareness
2. Keyboarding
3. Painting, drawing, and graphics
4. Multimedia/electronic presentations
5. CD-ROM
6. Network awareness
7. Internet/telecommunications
8. Databases/spreadsheets
9. Word processing
10. Desktop publishing

Teaching strategies/methodologies used:

The most effective methods of teaching technology use are:
- Demonstration and practice
- Lecture
- Modeling
- Guided and self-discovery
- Whole group and individualized

While these are not the only methodologies used, they are the most effective in a laboratory and classroom situation. The strategy selected is based on desired outcomes and the technology's design.

Resources, learning activities, assignments used to meet the varying needs of the students

Students use technology to practice curriculum skills, create meaning from classroom experiences, extend curriculum objectives, and re-mediate prior skills. Television and VCR use extends and supports the classroom curriculum as well as provides an opportunity to show computer-generated presentations to the whole class. Computer lab activities are designed to integrate computer skills with curriculum reinforcing activities. Additional technologies, including scanners, calculators and Internet connection, are also used to enhance the students' projects and add real-world connections to classroom lessons. Integrated learning activities are used to show that technology is only a tool to enrich the students' learning experiences. The following resources are available:

- A networked, Macintosh multimedia computer in each classroom with teacher-selected software specific to the grade's curriculum;
- CD-ROM encyclopedias in the library/media center and the computer lab networked printers;
- Curriculum-driven CD-ROM software in the computer lab for Grades K-2;
- High-speed Internet connections in every classroom and in the computer lab.

Questions and strategies used in classroom interaction

The types of questioning strategies used in the laboratory and classroom includes all levels of critical thinking.

- Knowledge: what, when, where, why, how.
- Comprehension: Tell in your own words, what does it

mean, compare and contrast.
- Application: how can you use it, where does it lead?
- Analysis: How would you begin, what are the causes, what are the problems?
- Evaluation: Which is the best solution, will it work, make a choice.
- Synthesis: Suppose, what if?

Grading policies used to evaluate student learning

Grading of computer lab activities for some grades is a combination of two grades. One grade, assigned by the classroom teacher, is based on mastery of the subject matter. The second grade, assigned by the computer teacher, is based on mastery of the computer skill. Any computer skill mastery grade is based on a 1 to 5 rubric grading system for each assignment or project:

- 1 = non-mastery of skill/software
- 2 = partial mastery of skill/software
- 3 = mastery of skill/software
- 4 = mastery with enhanced understanding of skill/software
- 5 = mastery with accelerated understanding of skill/software

This 1 to 5 ranking mirrors the marking codes in Grades Four through Eight. Grades One through Three marking codes mirror the 1,3,5 grading system. Students are also graded on effort and independent working skills. Several software programs are self-grading and provide immediate feedback to the students. These programs are used primarily in Kindergarten through Grade Three, with Grades Four through Eight using only one program with this design (keyboarding). These alternative assessments allow students to excel in curricular areas outside regular classroom learning situations. Therefore, with the help of technology, more students are able to succeed.

Instructional materials (including supplementary materials used to help the school achieve its stated goals and objectives in technology):

All software and hardware materials are chosen because of their ability to enhance students' use of technology. The software choices are made with the knowledge that curricular objectives will be met or enriched for the intended students. The use of Tech Works, a technology-skills program, enhances the planning of skills-based projects using classroom curriculum objectives to give substance to the project. The use of the Internet as a supplementary source of information and activities enriches the computer lab and classroom curriculum while also meeting several of the stated objectives in technology. Additional teacher supplementary materials, in the form of blackline masters and lesson suggestion workbooks, enable planning of projects that enhance classroom instruction.

Support for technology: library, resource room and computer room

The library is equipped with a one-server computer and five student machines that are fully networked for the computerized card catalog maintained by the librarian. The student computers are also connected to the Internet to serve as additional workstations for research opportunities. The librarian is experienced in online research techniques and helps students in their access to the necessary information. The library also has CD-ROM encyclopedias for use in updating hardcopy library materials.

The resource room, which is equipped with two multimedia computers, is used for: re-mediating skill deficiencies and facilitating new learning and problem-solving techniques; using technology as another method of presenting curriculum objectives to students who may not be successful in the typical classroom setting; and assessing curriculum skills through the use of self-graded software programs.

The computer lab is the primary facility for technology education. Each student in Grades One through Eight is scheduled for 45 minutes once a week in the computer lab. Students in kindergarten are scheduled for a twenty-minute session once a week. The computer lab has eighteen student computers networked to a server computer for shared access to peripherals, software and the Internet. The computer lab teacher works with classroom teachers to prepare curriculum enriching, computer skill-based activities and projects. The computer lab is available several periods a week for classroom teachers to plan computer time. Teachers can bring their classes to the lab for special activities outside of their regularly scheduled lab time. This additional access to the computer provides time for whole class instruction and activities. These opportunities also allow teachers another chance to incorporate technology into other curriculum areas.

Outcomes for Student Technology Use
All Students should have opportunities to demonstrate the following performances prior to the completion of Grade 2:

Indicators	Standard
Use input devices (mouse, keyboard, and remote control) and output devices (monitor and printer) to successfully operate computers, VCR's, audio tapes, and other technologies.	1
Use a variety of media and technology resources for directed and independent learning activities.	1,3
Communicate about technology using developmentally appropriate and accurate terminology	1
Use developmentally appropriate resources (interactive books, educational software, and elementary multimedia encyclopedias) to support learning	1
Work cooperatively and collaboratively with peers, family members, and others when using technology in the classroom.	2
Demonstrate positive social and ethical behaviors when using technology.	2
Practice responsible use of technology systems and software.	2
Create developmentally appropriate multimedia products with support from teachers, family members or student partners.	3
Use technology resources (puzzles, logical thinking programs, writing tools, digital cameras, drawing tools) for problem solving, communication, and illustration of thought, ideas, and stories.	3,4,5,6
Gather information and communicate with others using telecommunications, with support from teachers, family members, or student partners.	4

**All students should have opportunities to
demonstrate the following performances prior to
the completion of grade 5:**

Indicators	Standards
Use keyboards and other common input and output devices (including adaptive devices when necessary) efficiently and effectively.	1
Use a variety of media and technology resources for directed and independent learning activities	1,3
Communicate about technology using developmentally appropriate and accurate terminology.	1
Use developmentally appropriate resources (interactive books, educational software, and elementary multimedia encyclopedias) to support learning.	1
Work cooperatively and collaboratively with peers, family members, and others when using technology in the classroom.	2
Demonstrate positive social and ethical behaviors when using technology.	2
Practice responsible use of technology systems and software.	2
Create developmentally appropriate multimedia products with support from teachers, family members, or student partners.	3
Use technology resources (puzzles, logical thinking programs, writing tools, digital cameras, drawing tools) for problem solving, communication, and illustration of thought, ideas, and words.	3,4,5,6
Gather information and communicate with others using telecommunications, with support from teachers, family members, or student partners.	4

All students should have opportunities to demonstrate the following performances prior to the completion of Grade 8:

Indicators	Standard
Apply strategies for identifying and solving routine hardware and software problems that occur during everyday use.	1
Demonstrate knowledge and current changes in information technologies and the effect those changes have on the workplace and society.	2
Exhibit legal and ethical behaviors when using information and technology, and discuss consequences of misuse.	2
Use content-specific tools, software, and simulations (environmental probes, graphing calculators, exploratory environments, Web tools) to support learning and research.	3,5
Apply productivity/multimedia tools and peripherals to support personal productivity, group collaboration, and learning throughout the curriculum.	3,6
Design, develop, publish and present products (web pages, videotapes) using technology resources that demonstrate and communicate curriculum concepts to audiences inside and outside the classroom.	4,5,6
Collaborate with peers, experts, and others using telecommunications and collaborative tools to investigate curriculum-related problems, issues, and information, and to develop solutions or products for audiences inside and outside the classroom.	4,5
Select and use appropriate tools and technology resources to accomplish a variety of tasks and solve problems.	5,6
Demonstrate an understanding of concepts underlying hardware, software, connectivity, and of practical applications to learning and problem solving.	1,6
Research and evaluate the accuracy, relevance, appropriateness, comprehensiveness, and bias of electronic information sources concerning real world problems.	2,5,6

CURRICULUM DRIVES THE USAGE OF TECHNOLOGY

KATHLEEN KILEY, ASSISTANT PRINCIPAL
ANNUNCIATION CATHOLIC ACADEMY
ALTAMONTE SPRINGS, FLORIDA

TECHNOLOGY IN THE CLASSROOM

In order to prepare our students for the new millennium, we must give them the skills to manage and manipulate information, learn how to work in collaborative teams, and be creative problem solvers. True integration of technology in schools avoids merely substituting computers for traditional methods of teaching. It involves using computers efficiently and effectively so students can apply computer skills in a meaningful way. The computer is an important learning tool, but it is the curriculum that should drive technology usage. Software should be selected carefully to complement the curriculum and the arrangement of the classroom should be carefully planned.

Schools should have a vision of how technology will improve their curriculum. There should be a clear technology plan that outlines, step-by-step, how the objectives will be accomplished.

TEACHER TRAINING

Teachers are an essential element in a successful integration program. If they are not excited about using technology, computers will be underused or unused. Instructional changes occur gradually and so do struggles with new technologies. There are many things, however, that an administrator can do to help generate enthusiasm among the teachers. For example, they can:

- Give teachers needed time for exploration and development;
- Provide substitute teachers for those faculty members who want to explore in-house collections of CD's or other computer programs;
- Provide time for teachers during the week to work together

- with team members to plan technological applications and time with a technology coordinator to answer questions;
- Provide speakers and workshops for teachers with lots of hands-on experience;
- Use some time during faculty meetings for teachers to share innovative methods they have used to integrate technology into the classroom;
- Pair a new teacher with a "cyber buddy" who will guide him/her and insure that he/she doesn't become overwhelmed;
- Set up a gradual timeline outlining when certain programs should be mastered. This will help ease apprehension for new teachers;
- Model behavior by using technology in all aspects of their job. Training should be an ongoing process for everyone.

COMPUTER APPLICATIONS

The computer can be a very productive tool in the classroom. It can be used as a word processor, database, spreadsheet and desktop publisher. Spreadsheets can help students explore mathematical relationships and formulas. Desktop publishing allows students to combine text and graphics to produce high quality products. They can create newsletter, signs and banners. Computers can be used to facilitate and improve instruction. **Computer-Assisted Instruction (CAI)** programs use tutorials and drill and practice simulations as well as test students' understanding. These programs allow students to work at their own pace and help teachers individualize instruction. CAI programs produce simulations modeled after real life experiences. *The Oregon Trail* and *SimCity* are good examples of simulation programs. In *The Oregon Trail*, students travel to Oregon as emigrants did in 1840 and face all the same hardships. *SimCity* teaches students about critical issues involved in building and managing a city. **Computer-Managed Instruction (CMI)** differs from CAI in that it focuses on the needs of the teachers. CMI programs keeps track of students' attendance, grades, schedules, and can assign different programs to different students. The CMI program can make the classroom teacher more organized and productive.

The word "multimedia" is often heard in educational settings. Multimedia refers to communication from more than one media source such as text, audio, graphics, animated graphics, and full-motion video. When students work on a multimedia project, they learn both content and computer skills. These projects can teach students about terminology: stacks, buttons, textbox, graphic, navigate, scroll and the skills needed to create multimedia presentations: storyboards, text and graphic boxes, and adding transitions. Children also discover that they can create projects, work with others in a group, and meet deadlines. Students can use electronic encyclopedias and the Internet for research and analyze and synthesize that information into a presentation. HyperStudio and Microsoft's PowerPoint are two software programs that have been used successfully in schools.

ELECTRONIC ASSESSMENT

Using the computer for testing has advantages for both teacher and student. No more long lines for teachers at the copy machine and no more using reams of paper for testing. The teacher is freed up from test correction and can use this time to work with students. Students enjoy taking on-line tests because they receive immediate feedback since most programs require the student to get the right answer before continuing. Also, students have more flexibility since they can take a test when they have mastered the material. When a child takes an on-line test, they not only demonstrate what they have learned in the content area, but they can also learn how to retrieve and send e-mail, highlight, copy, paste, make tables, print, and a wide variety of other computer-related tasks. All of this can be accomplished in one activity.

INTERNET USAGE AT SCHOOL

Internet access can lead students to the best of everything and the worst of everything. It would be a shame, however, if students missed out on all the good things the Internet has to offer just because of the existence of some inappropriate sites. It is important to teach our students about Internet safety and to be aware of potential parental concerns. If we are prudent when using the Internet at school, we can reap the overwhelming benefits that it has to offer. The Internet creates a global community of learners, exposes our students to other kinds of thinking, and broadens our curricular scope to include new methodologies and strategies.

Schools across America are hooking up to the Internet at a rapid pace. They are finding that the ability to access virtually unlimited resources is both a benefit and a burden. Using the Internet as an educational tool can facilitate communication with classrooms around the world, give students the access to a multitude of library databases, link the students with experts in their fields of study, expedite research, and provide other innumerable resources. On the other hand, school administrators realize that the Internet is impossible to censor and control completely. Administrators are not naïve to the inappropriate material their students can view either accidentally or deliberately. Parental concern and response to Internet access can range from outrage to indifference.

PARENTAL CONCERNS WITH THE INTERNET

Parents often seek to influence school policies when programs providing sensitive information are introduced. With the advent of interactive technology that is now available to school children, questions about appropriateness and adequate supervision have already touched off debate among parents and school leaders.

Educators know the available information and applications of the computer-based educational software that their schools have purchased, but this cannot be said about the Internet. Students can be exposed to inappropriate material and become involved in spontaneous interaction with others online. As an educational tool, the Internet will likely expose schools to significant challenges for many years, especially because the content available to children is not capable of being controlled fully by schools.

Parents have expressed their concerns about computer systems that would use the Internet to link parents with the school. The program would provide parents with access to their children's test scores, attendance records, and teacher remarks. Despite the fact that access would require a password and the student's identification number, confidentiality concerns were raised.

PROTECTING YOUR SCHOOL AGAINST LIABILITY WHEN USING THE INTERNET

Every school should have a clearly written Acceptable Use Policy (AUP), which should be signed as a prerequisite to computer use. The more specific the language of an AUP, the more effective it will prove as both a management and educational tool. The AUP defines acceptable use of electronic information and minimizes institutional liability. The AUP should cover what the user can and cannot do online and explain the consequences for violating the agreement. The statement should clearly identify the school's expectations for students' behavior. The more an AUP can refer to the school's established behavior codes, the stronger the policy will be and the more readily understood.

A commercial filtering device is one way schools can restrict students' access to the Internet. Through this device they can filter out potentially harmful materials. The filters block access to Internet sites that contain certain words or phrases. There is much controversy, however, surrounding filters. Filtering devices are expensive and can give a false sense of security to school administrators.

Other suggestions for online safety include: requiring parental permission before allowing students to go online; providing students with passwords; and not allowing students to enter chat rooms.

When it comes to student safety on the net, there is no substitute for close supervision. Students should log on to the Internet with a set educational objective. Ideally, teachers should pre-screen sites and students should be instructed to only use those sites. Schools are responsible for educating students on Internet usage. This education should include "netiquette" and should describe what to do in the event they find themselves on an inappropriate site. With proper instruction, students should feel comfortable to explore the wonder and power of the Internet.

Controversies surrounding the student use of the Internet are bound to increase as the numbers of students going online increases. Schools should make efforts to reduce the likelihood of their students accessing inappropriate material and they should punish students fairly who violate school Internet policy. Students should not be discouraged from going online.

CONCLUSION

The most important component when integrating technology into the curriculum is the classroom teacher. Teachers understand why basic technology competencies are important. Dedicated teachers know how to integrate technology using a consistent and well-designed model of instruction. True integration comes when students learn through computers, not about them. There is no value in learning computer skills unless they are used to further content comprehension. How classroom teachers of the twenty-first century implement computers into their schools is critical to achieving the benefits of technology in children's learning. Well-trained and competent teachers of the next century will make integration a success. By understanding this, teachers of the twenty-first century will meet the challenge of preparing students to become critical thinkers, proficient information handlers, and creative problem solvers.

REFERENCES

Bernauer, J. October (1996). "The Power of Partnering." *Technology Horizons in Education.* Vol. 24, No. 3, p. 71.
Butzin, S. December (1992). "Integrating Technology into the Classroom." *Phi Delta Kappan*, Vol. 74, No. 4, p. 330.
Dockstader, J. January (1999). "Teachers of the 21st Century Know the What, Why, and How of Integration." *Technological Horizons in Education.* Vol. 26, p. 6.
Dyril, O., Kinnamon, D. February (1994). "Integrating Technology in Into Your Classroom Curriculum." *Technology & Learning*, Vol 14, No. 5, p. 38.
Sharp, V. (1999). *Computer Education for Teachers.*